Practical Guide to the Operational Use of the Glock Pistol
By Erik Lawrence
Copyright ©2015 Erik Lawrence

All rights reserved. No part of this book may be reproduced or transmitted in any form or by any means, electronic or mechanical, including photocopying, recording, or by an information storage and retrieval system, without permission in writing from the publisher. Exceptions to this include reviewers who may quote brief passages in a review to be printed in a magazine, newspaper, or on the Internet. For information, please contact:

Erik Lawrence
www.vig-sec.com   erik@vig-sec.com

Although the author and publisher have made every effort to ensure the accuracy and completeness of information contained in this book, we assume no responsibility for the use or misuse of information contained in this book and errors, inaccuracies, omissions, or any inconsistency herein. Portions of this manual are excerpts from outside sources but been validated and modified as necessary.

Printed and bound in the United States of America

First printing 2015

ISBN 13: 978-1-941998-76-2
Ebook ISBN 13: 978-1-941998-77-9

ATTENTION US MILITARY UNITS, US GOVERNMENT AGENCIES, AND PROFESSIONAL ORGANIZATIONS: Quantity discounts are available on bulk purchases of this book. Special books or book excerpts can also be created to fit specific needs. For information, please contact

Erik Lawrence

www.vig-sec.com   erik@vig-sec.com

Firearms are potentially dangerous and must be handled responsibly by individuals. The technical information presented in this manual on the use of the Glock pistol reflects the author's research, beliefs, and experiences. The information in this book is presented for academic study only. Neither the author nor the publisher assumes any responsibility for the use or misuse of information contained in this book.

SAFETY NOTICE
Before starting an inspection, ensure the weapon is cleared. Do not manipulate the trigger until the weapon has been cleared of all ammunition. Inspect the chamber to ensure that it is empty and no ammunition is present. Keep the weapon oriented in a safe direction when loading and handling.

AMMUNITION NOTICE This weapon fires the several different calibers, so be sure know which model of pistol you are using and match the ammunition accordingly. Firing the incorrect ammunition will damage the weapon and possibly injure the operator.

Training should be received from knowledgeable and experienced operators on this particular weapons system. Vigilant Security Services, LLC® provides this training and continually perfects its instruction with up-to-date information from actual use.

www.vig-sec.com

Table of Contents

Section 1 1
  Introduction 1
    Background 1
    Design 2
    Operation 4
    Variants 6
    Magazines 34

Section 2 35
  Maintenance 35
  Clearing the Glock 35
    Disassembling the Glock Pistol 37
    Inspecting the Glock 43
    Reassembling the Field-stripped Glock Pistol 48
    Performing a Function Check on the Glock Pistol 50
    Safeties on a Glock 51
    Sights 53
    Troubleshooting 54

Section 3 57
  Operation and Function 57
    Loading the Glock Magazine 57
    Loading the Glock Pistol 58
    Firing the Glock Pistol 59

Section 4 61
  Performance Problems 61
    Malfunction and Immediate Action Procedures 61

Appendix A – Accessories for Glock Pistols 70
Appendix B – Holsters, Magazine Pouches, and Lights 74

Section 1

Introduction

The objective of this manual is to allow the reader to be able to use the various Glock pistols competently. The manual will give the reader background/specifications of the weapon; instructions on its operation, disassembly, and assembly; proper firing procedure; and malfunction/misfire procedures. Operator-level maintenance will also be detailed to allow the reader to understand and become competent in the use and maintenance of the Glock pistol.

Background

The company started as a manufacturer of curtain rods and then branched out into supplying the Austrian army with machine gun belts, practice hand grenades, plastic magazines, field knives, and entrenching tools.

GLOCK was founded by Mr. Gaston Glock, an engineer, in 1963 in Deutsch-Wagram near Vienna to specialize in the manufacture of plastic and steel components. In the early 1980s, the Austrian military decided to acquire a new duty pistol, asking numerous famous local and foreign weapon manufacturers for their bids. Due to Glock's excellent reputation with previous military contracts, GLOCK was also invited to bid on this new contract. This was a new challenge for the company, since pistols were not in its product line at that time. The result was a breakthrough in firearms technology. With its polymer frame, the GLOCK pistol was considerably lighter in weight and had the highest magazine capacity of any other pistol in its class. The pistol did not have any external safety lever, hammer, decocker, or any other operation controls which must be deactivated prior to making the weapon ready to shoot. In this way, the pistol was faster, simpler, and safer to use than any other pistol. The new pistol concept allowed the shooter to concentrate on tactical considerations rather than on manipulation of levers or hammers on the pistol. In short, the pistol combined two different systems – it considered the advantages of the double-action revolver (simple to operate, reliable) and those of the auto-loading pistol (maximum firepower, fast reloading). This combination was the birth of the well-known Safe-Action system. By merely pulling the trigger to the rear, the three independent safeties (trigger safety, firing pin safety, and drop safety) are automatically deactivated and re-activated when the trigger is released.

In 1985, an important milestone was achieved with the establishment of GLOCK, Inc., in Smyrna, Georgia, to address the firearms market in the United States. The so-called "wonder-nine" GLOCK 17 met with immediate approval and overwhelming acceptance in the law enforcement and civilian markets. The success of the GLOCK pistol made it necessary to open a second subsidiary in Hong Kong in 1988 to address the Asian and Australian markets. Consequently, the production capacity was enlarged by a second factory in Ferlach/Carinthia in Austria.

Its first handgun model was the Glock 17, a 9mm Luger Parabellum semi-automatic pistol with a magazine capacity of 17 rounds (unusually large at the time), introduced in the early 1980s as a response to the Austrian army's request for a new sidearm. Glock pistols are popular with law enforcement agencies, the military, security personnel, and defense-minded private citizens. Glock was the first manufacturer to offer models chambered in the .40 S&W cartridge (Glock 22 & Glock 23 – 1990), beating Smith & Wesson to the marketplace with their own cartridge. The Glock 22 is currently the single most popular police sidearm in use in the United States.

Glock also offers pistols chambered in .357 SIG, .380 ACP, 10mm Auto, .45 ACP, and the new .45 GAP (Glock Automatic Pistol). A very rare run of 9x21mm Glock 19 pistols were made. Glock .380 pistols are not currently available in the United States due to the BATFE's point system. "C" models are built with a "compensator" feature to reduce recoil.

Glock side arms are very common handguns among law enforcement agencies and military organizations around the world. They are standard-issue side arms for the Austrian, Belgian, Dutch, and Norwegian armies; Austrian and Northern Irish police forces; and various special units, such as the German GSG 9 counter-terrorism unit of the German Federal Police and Specialist Firearms Command of the London Metropolitan Police Service, as well as the new Iraq security forces.

Design

The Glock is a locked breech, short recoil pistol, chambered in 9mm Luger, .40 Smith and Wesson, .357 SIG, .380 ACP, 10mm Auto, .45 ACP, and includes the new .45 GAP (Glock Automatic Pistol) semi-automatic pistol. It uses a modified Petter/Browning barrel locking system.

Prior to 1982, it was considered impossible to manufacture a pistol with a polymer grip. All prejudice was rapidly refuted when GLOCK pistols proved to be many times more durable than conventional pistols.

In addition to a 90% savings in weight, minimum thermal conductivity, and steady firing characteristics, the GLOCK frame is ergonomically ideal. The GLOCK hi-tech polymer does not include glass fiber reinforcement, resulting in unsurpassed breaking strength in the cold.

Solid, cold-hammered barrels with Tenifer surface treatment and rounded (hexagonal or octagonal) interior profiles offer numerous advantages to the user. GLOCK barrels are considerably easier to clean and maintain uniform precision, even after a high number of rounds.

The user has always been able to read important parameters off his Glock pistol at a glance.
- Trigger forward = safety activated
- Trigger pulled = safety deactivated

The pistol also shows the user whether a cartridge is or is not in the barrel. The extractor additionally serves as a loaded chamber indicator on all Glock pistols – and this feature entirely without additional components.

Glock offers the user the possibility of modular-mounting a wide range of weapon accessories on his pistol. On non-subcompact models is a Picatinny rail under the front of the receiver to attach light and lasers.

Glock pistols use an internal safety mechanism with three components, with no external thumb-activated safety switch as might be found on traditional-design pistols. Glock calls this the "Safe Action" system. All three safeties are disabled, one after the other, when the trigger is depressed. They are
- Trigger Safety: An external lever mechanism contained within the trigger prevents the trigger from moving unless the lever is depressed.
- Striker Safety: A spring-loaded pin attached by an extension bar to the trigger assembly blocks the striker from striking the primer of the cartridge until the trigger is pulled.
- Drop Safety: The far end of the same extension bar locks the striker into place from the rear until the trigger is pulled.

Similar systems for internal safeties have since become standard for many major manufacturers of semi-automatic pistols. However, Glock pistols, like any other firearm, can discharge and cause injury or death if the operator accidentally or negligently manipulates the trigger. The absence of a traditional safety switch means that Glock users who intend to carry the gun on their person with the chamber loaded must be cautious (as they should be with any type of firearm) of keeping their finger off of the trigger when holstering or unholstering the gun.

In 2003, Glock announced the Internal Locking System (ILS). The ILS is a manually activated lock that is located in the back of the pistol's grip. It is cylindrical in design and, according to Glock, each key is unique. Group key hierarchic solutions are available for law enforcement agencies. When activated, the lock causes a tab to protrude from the rear of the grip, giving both a visual and tactile indication as to whether or not the lock is engaged. When activated, the ILS renders the Glock unfireable and makes it impossible to disassemble. When disengaged, the ILS adds no further safety mechanisms to the Glock pistol. The ILS is available as an option on all Glock pistols except for the G36, but not all ILS-equipped Glock pistols are carried by distributors nor imported with the option.

The Glock Tenifer process optimizes the molecular structure of the metal surfaces, achieving a degree of hardness which comes close to that of diamond. The Tenifer finish is a hi-tech surface refinement for the barrel and slide that allows for minimum corrosion and provides an anti-reflective finish.

Operation

Safe-Action Trigger System

The "Safe Action" system is a partly tensioned firing pin lock, which is moved further back by the trigger bar when the trigger is pulled. When the trigger is pulled, three safety features are automatically deactivated, one after another. When doing so, the trigger bar is deflected downward by the connector, and the firing pin is released under full load. When the trigger is released, all three safety features re-engage, and the GLOCK pistol is automatically secured again.

The Glock Safe Action system is neither single action (SA) nor double action (DA). The Glock, unlike most center fire handguns, does not have a hammer which is dropped to push a firing pin when the trigger is pulled. Instead, the Glock has a striker which is completely enclosed within the slide. Whenever a round is in the chamber, the striker is partially retracted under tension. There isn't enough tension to fire the gun if for some reason the striker were forced forward from this position.

- **Single Action** (SA): Pulling the trigger performs a single function, releasing the hammer or striker.
- **Double Action** (DA): Pulling the trigger performs two actions, cocking the hammer or striker and then releasing it.
- **Safe Action**: Pulling the trigger completes the striker cocking and then releases it.

When the shooter pulls the trigger, the striker is retracted the rest of the way to full tension, from which it can fire the gun. Because the trigger action need only retract the striker part way, the trigger stroke is shorter and lighter than traditional DA designs.

The biggest advantage of the Safe Action system is that the trigger pull is consistent from shot to shot. Unlike DA/SA guns, which fire their first shot with a long, heavy DA stroke and subsequent shots with lighter, shorter strokes, the Glock pull never changes. Glocks come standard with 5½-pound triggers, but a certified armorer can increase it to 8 or 11 pounds. A 3½-pound trigger option is also available on certain competition models and from aftermarket retailers. SA and DAO (double-action only) guns share this feature, but SA guns require the shooter to disengage a safety switch before firing, and DAO guns have significantly heavier trigger pulls (9 pounds or more).

Variants

Glock 17/17C

Figure 1-1a Glock 17 Pistol   Figure 1-1b Glock 17C Pistol

NSN 1005-17-144-3969 (Glock 17)

Caliber	9mm (9x19mm)
Magazine Capacity	17 rounds – standard; 19 or 33 rounds also available
Overall Length	7.32"/186mm
Height (Including Mag)	5.43"/138mm
Width	1.18"/ 30mm
Sight Radius	6.49"/165mm
Barrel Length	4.49"/114mm
Barrel Rifling	Right, Hexagonal
Length of Twist	9.84"/250mm
Weight (Without Mag)	22.04 oz/625g (G17)/21.87oz/605g (G17C)
Empty Mag Weight	2.75 oz/78g
Full Mag Weight	9.87 oz/280g
Trigger Pull	5.5 lbs/2.5kg
Trigger Travel	0.5"/12.5mm
Action	Glock Safe Action

Glock 17L

Figure 1-2 Glock 17L Pistol

Caliber	9mm (9x19mm)
Magazine Capacity	17 rounds
Overall Length	8.85"/225mm
Height (Including Mag)	5.43"/138mm
Width	1.18"/30mm
Sight Radius	8.07"/205mm
Barrel Length	6.02"/153mm
Barrel Rifling	Right, Hexagonal
Length of Twist	9.84"/250mm
Weight (Without Mag)	23.63 oz/670g
Empty Mag Weight	2.75 oz/78g
Full Mag Weight	9.87 oz/280g
Trigger Pull	4.5 lbs/2.0kg
Trigger Travel	0.5"/12.5mm
Action	Glock Safe Action

The "L" in Glock 17L stands for longslide. The G17L is 1.5 inches longer than the G17, with a corresponding longer barrel. Because of its extended length, the G17L is mainly used for competition.

Glock 18/18C

Figure 1-3 Glock 18C Pistol

Caliber	9mm (9x19mm)
Operating Modes	Semi-automatic and Full-automatic
Magazine Capacity	17 rounds – standard; 33 rounds also available
Overall Length	7.32"/186mm
Height (Including Mag)	5.43"/138mm
Width	1.18"/ 30mm
Sight Radius	6.49"/165mm
Barrel Length	4.49"/114mm
Barrel Rifling	Right, Hexagonal
Length of Twist	9.84"/250mm
Weight (Without Mag)	22.04 oz/625g (G18)/21.87oz/605g (G18C)
Empty Mag Weight	2.75 oz/78g
Full Mag Weight	9.87 oz/280g
Trigger Pull	5.5 lbs/2.5kg
Trigger Travel	0.5"/12.5mm
Action	Glock Safe Action

Glock 19/19C

Figure 1-4a Glock 19 Pistol

Figure 1-4b Glock 19C Pistol

NSN 1005-66-132-7731 (Glock 19)

Caliber	9mm (9x19mm)
Magazine Capacity	15 rounds – standard; 17, 19, or 33 rounds also available
Overall Length	6.85"/174mm
Height (Including Mag)	5.00"/127mm
Width	1.18"/30mm
Sight Radius	6.02"/153mm
Barrel Length	4.02"/102mm
Barrel Rifling	Right, Hexagonal
Length of Twist	9.84"/250mm
Weight (Without Mag)	20.99 oz/595 g (G19)/20.67oz/586g (G19C)
Empty Mag Weight	2.46 oz/70g
Full Mag Weight	8.99 oz/255g
Trigger Pull	5.5 lbs/2.5kg
Trigger Travel	0.5"/12.5mm
Action	Glock Safe Action

Glock 20/20C

Figure 1-5a Glock 20 Pistol

Figure 1-5b Glock 20C Pistol

Caliber	10mm
Magazine Capacity	15 rounds
Overall Length	7.59"/193mm
Height (Including Mag)	5.47"/139mm
Width	1.27"/32.5mm
Sight Radius	6.77"/172mm
Barrel Length	4.60"/117mm
Barrel Rifling	Right, Hexagonal
Length of Twist	9.84"/250mm
Weight (Without Mag)	27.68 oz/785g (G20)/27.34 oz/775g (G20C)
Empty Mag Weight	2.64 oz/75g
Full Mag Weight	11.46 oz/325g
Trigger Pull	5.5 lbs/2.5kg
Trigger Travel	0.5"/12.5mm
Action	Glock Safe Action

Glock 21/21C

Figure 1-6a Glock 21 Pistol

Figure 1-6b Glock 21C Pistol

Caliber	.45 Automatic (ACP)
Magazine Capacity	13 rounds
Overall Length	7.59"/193mm
Height (Including Mag)	5.47"/139mm
Width	1.27"/32.5mm
Sight Radius	6.77"/172mm
Barrel Length	4.60"/117mm
Barrel Rifling	Right, Octagonal
Length of Twist	15.75"/400mm
Weight (Without Mag)	26.28 oz/745g (G21)/25.93 oz/735g (G21C)
Empty Mag Weight	3.1 oz/88g
Full Mag Weight	12.0 oz/340g
Trigger Pull	5.5 lbs/2.5kg
Trigger Travel	0.5"/12.5mm
Action	Glock Safe Action

Glock 21SF

Figure 1-7 Glock 21 SF Pistol

Caliber	.45 ACP
Magazine Capacity	13 rounds
Overall Length	7.59"/193mm
Height (Including Mag)	5.47"/139mm
Width	1.27"/32.5mm
Sight Radius	6.77"/172mm
Barrel Length	4.60"/117mm
Barrel Rifling	Right, Octagonal
Length of Twist	15.75"/400mm
Weight (Without Mag)	26.28 oz/745g
Empty Mag Weight	3.1 oz/88g
Full Mag Weight	12.0 oz/340g
Trigger Pull	5.5 lbs/2.5kg
Trigger Travel	0.5"/12.5mm
Action	Glock Safe Action

- Ambidextrous mag release
- Glock or Picatinny rail
- Uses a slightly modified G21 13-round magazine

Glock 22/22C

Figure 1-8a Glock 22 Pistol

Figure 1-8b Glock 22C Pistol

Caliber	.40 Smith and Wesson
Magazine Capacity	15 rounds
Overall Length	7.32"/186mm
Height (Including Mag)	5.43"/138mm
Width	1.18"/30mm
Sight Radius	6.49"/165mm
Barrel Length	4.49"/114mm
Barrel Rifling	Right, Hexagonal
Length of Twist	9.84"/250mm
Weight (Without Mag)	22.92 oz/650g (G22)/22.54 oz/725g (G22C)
Empty Mag Weight	2.75 oz/78g
Full Mag Weight	11.46 oz/325g
Trigger Pull	5.5 lbs/2.5kg
Trigger Travel	0.5"/12.5mm
Action	Glock Safe Action

Figure 1-8c Glock Compensator when fired

Glock 23/23C

Figure 1-9a Glock 23 Pistol

Figure 1-9b Glock 23C Pistol

Caliber	.40 Smith and Wesson
Magazine Capacity	13 rounds
Overall Length	6.85"/174mm
Height (Including Mag)	5.00"/127mm
Width	1.18"/30mm
Sight Radius	6.02"/153mm
Barrel Length	4.02"/102mm
Barrel Rifling	Right, Hexagonal
Length of Twist	9.84"/250mm
Weight (Without Mag)	21.16 oz/600g (G23)/20.95 oz/590g (G23C)
Empty Mag Weight	2.46 oz/70g
Full Mag Weight	9.87 oz/280g
Trigger Pull	5.5 lbs/2.5kg
Trigger Travel	0.5"/12.5mm
Action	Glock Safe Action

Glock 24/24C

Figure 1-10a Glock 24 Pistol   Figure 1-10b Glock 24C Pistol

Caliber	.40 Smith and Wesson
Magazine Capacity	15 rounds
Overall Length	8.85"/225mm
Height (Including Mag)	5.43"/138mm
Width	1.18"/30mm
Sight Radius	8.07"/205mm
Barrel Length	6.02"/153mm
Barrel Rifling	Right, Hexagonal
Length of Twist	9.84"/250mm
Weight (Without Mag)	26.70 oz/757g (G24)/26.7 oz/747g (G24C)
Empty Mag Weight	2.75 oz/78g
Full Mag Weight	11.46 oz/325g
Trigger Pull	4.5 lbs/2.0kg
Trigger Travel	0.5"/12.5mm
Action	Glock Safe Action

Glock 25

Figure 1-11 Glock 25 Pistol

Caliber	.380 ACP
Magazine Capacity	15 rounds
Overall Length	6.85"/174mm
Height (Including Mag)	5.00"/127mm
Width	1.18"/30mm
Sight Radius	6.02"/153mm
Barrel Length	4.02"/102mm
Barrel Rifling	Right, Hexagonal
Length of Twist	9.84"/250mm
Weight (Without Mag)	20.11 oz/570g
Empty Mag Weight	2.40 oz/68g
Full Mag Weight	7.20 oz/204g
Trigger Pull	5.5 lbs/2.5kg
Trigger Travel	0.5"/12.5mm
Action	Glock Safe Action

Glock 26

Figure 1-12 Glock 26 Pistol

Caliber	9mm (9x19mm)
Magazine Capacity	10 rounds
Overall Length	6.29"/160mm
Height (Including Mag)	4.17"/106mm
Width	1.18"/30mm
Sight Radius	5.67"/144mm
Barrel Length	3.46"/88mm
Barrel Rifling	Right, Hexagonal
Length of Twist	9.84"/250mm
Weight (Without Mag)	19.75 oz/560g
Empty Mag Weight	1.98 oz/56g
Full Mag Weight	6.35 oz/180g
Trigger Pull	5.5 lbs/2.5kg
Trigger Travel	0.5"/12.5mm
Action	Glock Safe Action

Glock 27

Figure 1-13 Glock 27 Pistol

Caliber	.40 Smith and Wesson
Magazine Capacity	10 rounds
Overall Length	6.29"/160mm
Height (Including Mag)	4.17"/106mm
Width	1.18"/30mm
Sight Radius	5.67"/144mm
Barrel Length	3.46"/88mm
Barrel Rifling	Right, Hexagonal
Length of Twist	9.84"/250mm
Weight (Without Mag)	19.75 oz/560g
Empty Mag Weight	1.98 oz/56g
Full Mag Weight	6.35 oz/180g
Trigger Pull	5.5 lbs/2.5kg
Trigger Travel	0.5"/12.5mm
Action	Glock Safe Action

Glock 28

Figure 1-14 Glock 28 Pistol

Caliber	.380 ACP
Magazine Capacity	10 rounds
Overall Length	6.29"/160mm
Height (Including Mag)	4.17"/106mm
Width	1.18"/30mm
Sight Radius	5.67"/144mm
Barrel Length	3.46"/88mm
Barrel Rifling	Right, Hexagonal
Length of Twist	9.84"/250mm
Weight (Without Mag)	18.66 oz/529g
Empty Mag Weight	1.98 oz/56g
Full Mag Weight	5.11 oz/145g
Trigger Pull	5.5 lbs/2.5kg
Trigger Travel	0.5"/12.5mm
Action	Glock Safe Action

Glock 29

Figure 1-15 Glock 29 Pistol

Caliber	10mm
Magazine Capacity	10 rounds
Overall Length	6.77"/172mm
Height (Including Mag)	4.45"/113mm
Width	1.27"/32.5mm
Sight Radius	5.95"/151mm
Barrel Length	3.78"/96mm
Barrel Rifling	Right, Hexagonal
Length of Twist	9.84"/250mm
Weight (Without Mag)	24.69 oz/700g
Empty Mag Weight	2.40 oz/68g
Full Mag Weight	8.29 oz/235g
Trigger Pull	5.5 lbs/2.5kg
Trigger Travel	0.5"/12.5mm
Action	Glock Safe Action

Glock 30

Figure 1-16 Glock 30 Pistol

Caliber	.45 ACP
Magazine Capacity	10 rounds
Overall Length	6.77"/172mm
Height (Including Mag)	4.76"/121mm
Width	1.27"/32.5mm
Sight Radius	5.95"/151mm
Barrel Length	3.78"/96mm
Barrel Rifling	Right, Octagonal
Length of Twist	15.75"/400mm
Weight (Without Mag)	23.99 oz/680g
Empty Mag Weight	2.50 oz/71g
Full Mag Weight	9.87 oz/280g
Trigger Pull	5.5 lbs/2.5kg
Trigger Travel	0.5"/12.5mm
Action	Glock Safe Action

Glock 31/31C

Figure 1-17a Glock 31 Pistol

Figure 1-17b Glock 31C Pistol

Caliber	.357 Sig
Magazine Capacity	15 rounds
Overall Length	7.32"/186mm
Height (Including Mag)	5.43"/138mm
Width	1.18"/30mm
Sight Radius	6.49"/165mm
Barrel Length	4.49"/114mm
Barrel Rifling	Right, Hexagonal
Length of Twist	15.98"/406mm
Weight (Without Mag)	23.28 oz/660g (G31)/23.1 oz/650g (G31C)
Empty Mag Weight	2.75 oz/78g
Full Mag Weight	9.87 oz/280g
Trigger Pull	5.5 lbs/2.5kg
Trigger Travel	0.5"/12.5mm
Action	Glock Safe Action

Glock 32/32C

Figure 1-18a Glock 32 Pistol   Figure 1-18b Glock 32C Pistol

Caliber	.357 Sig
Magazine Capacity	13 rounds
Overall Length	6.85"/174mm
Height (Including Mag)	5.00"/127mm
Width	1.18"/30mm
Sight Radius	6.02"/153mm
Barrel Length	4.02"/102mm
Barrel Rifling	Right, Hexagonal
Length of Twist	15.98"/406mm
Weight (Without Mag)	21.52 oz/610g (G32)/21.34 oz/600g (G32C)
Empty Mag Weight	2.46 oz/70g
Full Mag Weight	8.64 oz/245g
Trigger Pull	5.5 lbs/2.5kg
Trigger Travel	0.5"/12.5mm
Action	Glock Safe Action

Glock 33

Figure 1-19 Glock 33 Pistol

Caliber	.357 Sig
Magazine Capacity	9 rounds
Overall Length	6.29"/160mm
Height (Including Mag)	4.17"/106mm
Width	1.18"/30mm
Sight Radius	5.67"/144mm
Barrel Length	3.46"/88mm
Barrel Rifling	Right, Hexagonal
Length of Twist	15.98"/406mm
Weight (Without Mag)	19.75 oz/560g
Empty Mag Weight	2.12 oz/60g
Full Mag Weight	6.88 oz/195g
Trigger Pull	5.5 lbs/2.5kg
Trigger Travel	0.5"/12.5mm
Action	Glock Safe Action

Glock 34

Figure 1-20 Glock 34 Pistol

Caliber	9mm (9x19mm)
Magazine Capacity	17 rounds
Overall Length	8.15"/207mm
Height (Including Mag)	5.43"/138mm
Width	1.18"/30mm
Sight Radius	7.56"/192mm
Barrel Length	5.32"/135mm
Barrel Rifling	Right, Hexagonal
Length of Twist	9.84"/250mm
Weight (Without Mag)	22.92 oz/650g
Empty Mag Weight	2.75 oz/78g
Full Mag Weight	9.87 oz/280g
Trigger Pull	4.5 lbs/2.0kg
Trigger Travel	0.5"/12.5mm
Action	Glock Safe Action

Glock 35

Figure 1-21 Glock 35 Pistol

Caliber	.40 Smith & Wesson
Magazine Capacity	15 rounds
Overall Length	8.15"/207mm
Height (Including Mag)	5.43"/138mm
Width	1.18"/30mm
Sight Radius	7.56"/192mm
Barrel Length	5.32"/135mm
Barrel Rifling	Right, Hexagonal
Length of Twist	9.84"/250mm
Weight (Without Mag)	24.52 oz/695g
Empty Mag Weight	2.75 oz/78g
Full Mag Weight	11.46 oz/325g
Trigger Pull	4.5 lbs/2.0kg
Trigger Travel	0.5"/12.5mm
Action	Glock Safe Action

Glock 36

Figure 1-22 Glock 36 Pistol

Caliber	.45 ACP
Magazine Capacity	6 rounds
Overall Length	6.77"/172mm
Height (Including Mag)	4.76"/121mm
Width	1.13"/28.5mm
Sight Radius	6.18"/157mm
Barrel Length	3.78"/96mm
Barrel Rifling	Right, Octagonal
Length of Twist	15.75"/400mm
Weight (Without Mag)	20.11 oz/570g
Empty Mag Weight	2.40 oz/68g
Full Mag Weight	6.88 oz/195g
Trigger Pull	5.5 lbs/2.5kg
Trigger Travel	0.5"/12.5mm
Action	Glock Safe Action

Glock 37

Figure 1-23 Glock 37 Pistol

Caliber	.45 GAP
Magazine Capacity	10 rounds
Overall Length	7.32"/186mm
Height (Including Mag)	5.51"/140mm
Width	1.18"/30mm
Sight Radius	6.49"/165mm
Barrel Length	4.49"/114mm
Barrel Rifling	Right, Octagonal
Length of Twist	15.75"/400mm
Weight (Without Mag)	25.95 oz/735g
Empty Mag Weight	2.68 oz/76g
Full Mag Weight	9.53 oz/270g
Trigger Pull	5.5 lbs/2.5kg
Trigger Travel	0.5"/12.5mm
Action	Glock Safe Action

Glock 38

Figure 1-24 Glock 38 Pistol

Caliber	.45 GAP
Magazine Capacity	8 rounds
Overall Length	6.85"/174mm
Height (Including Mag)	5.00"/127mm
Width	1.18"/30mm
Sight Radius	6.02"/153mm
Barrel Length	4.02"/102mm
Barrel Rifling	Right, Octagonal
Length of Twist	15.75"/400mm
Weight (Without Mag)	24.16 oz/685g
Trigger Pull	5.5 lbs/2.5kg
Trigger Travel	0.5"/12.5mm
Action	Glock Safe Action

Glock 39

Figure 1-25 Glock 39 Pistol

Caliber	.45 GAP
Magazine Capacity	6 rounds
Overall Length	6.30"/160mm
Height (Including Mag)	4.17"/127mm
Width	1.18"/30mm
Sight Radius	5.67"/144mm
Barrel Length	3.46"/88mm
Barrel Rifling	Right, Octagonal
Length of Twist	15.75"/400mm
Weight (Without Mag)	19.33 oz/548g
Trigger Pull	5.5 lbs/2.5kg
Trigger Travel	0.5"/12.5mm
Action	Glock Safe Action

Glock 40 Gen 4

Figure 1-25 Glock 40 Gen 4 Pistol

Caliber	10mm Auto
Magazine Capacity	15 rounds
Overall Length	9.49"/241mm
Height (Including Mag)	5.28"/139mm
Width	1.28"/32.5mm
Sight Radius	8.19"/208mm
Barrel Length	6.02"/153mm
Barrel Rifling	Right, Octagonal
Length of Twist	9.84"/250mm
Weight (Without Mag)	28.15 oz/798g
Trigger Pull	5.5 lbs/2.5kg
Trigger Travel	0.5"/12.5mm
Action	Glock Safe Action

Glock 41 Gen 4

Figure 1-26 Glock 41 Gen 4 Pistol

Caliber	.45 ACP
Magazine Capacity	13 rounds
Overall Length	8.9"/226mm
Height (Including Mag)	5.47"/139mm
Width	1.28"/32.5mm
Sight Radius	7.56"/192mm
Barrel Length	5.31"/135mm
Barrel Rifling	Right, Octagonal
Length of Twist	15.75"/400mm
Weight (Without Mag)	27 oz/765g
Trigger Pull	5.5 lbs/2.5kg
Trigger Travel	0.5"/12.5mm
Action	Glock Safe Action

Glock 42

Figure 1-27 Glock 42 Pistol

Caliber	.380 ACP
Magazine Capacity	6 rounds
Overall Length	5.94"/151mm
Height (Including Mag)	4.13"/105mm
Width	0.94"/24mm
Sight Radius	4.92"/125mm
Barrel Length	3.25"/82.5mm
Barrel Rifling	Right, Octagonal
Length of Twist	9.84"/250mm
Weight (Without Mag)	13.76 oz/390g
Trigger Pull	5.5 lbs/2.5kg
Trigger Travel	0.5"/12.5mm
Action	Glock Safe Action

Magazines

Like no other pistol, Glock pistols permit almost unrestricted compatibility of the magazines within a caliber. Standard magazines, for instance, can also be used for backup weapons. Compact and subcompact Glock pistol model magazines can be loaded with a convincing number of rounds – i.e., Glock 26 with up to 33 rounds.

The innovative polymer frame of the Glock pistol does not require grip shells. As a result, it has considerably more space for the magazine body and enables a double-row staggered cartridge configuration.

Glock magazines have a stiff metal tube encased in the proven Glock high-tech polymer. This configuration resists deformation – even when dropped from great height or exposed to extreme environmental conditions. Magazines with extended floor plates (plus 2 rounds) are available in calibers 9x19, .40, .380, and .357 Sig.

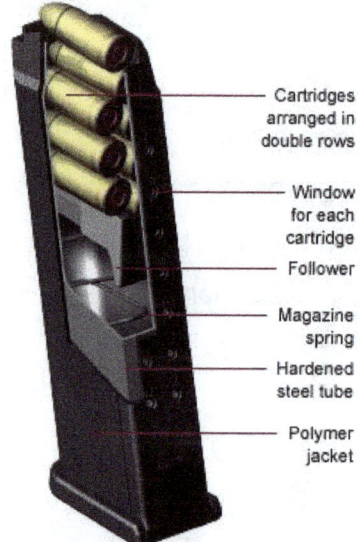

Figure 1-28 Magazine cutaway view

Figure 1-29 33-round 9mm magazine

Section 2

Maintenance

Clearing the Glock

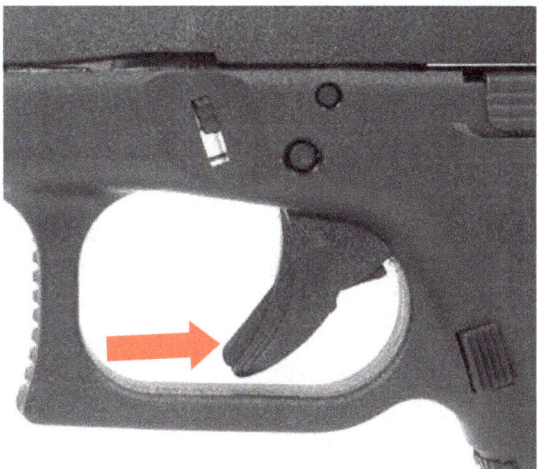

Figure 2-1 Glock external safety

A. Ensure the pistol is pointed in a safe direction and finger is off the trigger and out of the trigger guard.

Figure 2-2a
Depress the magazine release

Figure 2-2b
Remove the magazine

B. Remove the magazine by pressing the magazine catch to the right (Figure 2-2a) and pull the magazine from the magazine well in the grip Figure 2-2b). You may have to pull on the front lip of the magazine to free it. Place the magazine in a pocket or magazine pouch or set it down.

Figure 2-3a
Hold onto the serrations and pull.

Figure 2-3b
Press up on the slide stop.

C. 1- Grip the serrations on the slide (Figure 2-3a) and 2- pull the slide rearward, allowing the round to extract and eject from the pistol. 3- Press up on the slide stop and release the tension on the slide to lock the slide to the rear (Figure 2-3b). Observe the round extracting and ejecting from the ejection port; do not attempt to retain the round.

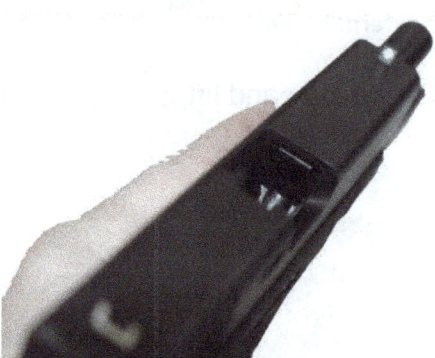
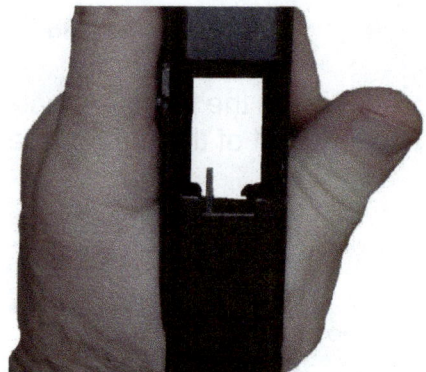

Figure 2-4
Check the chamber.

Figure 2-5
Check the ejector.

D. Visually check the chamber for a round (Figure 2-4). Once you have ensured the pistol has no magazine in it, the ejector is not damaged, (Figure 2-5), and the chamber is free of ammunition, you now can close the slide by pulling the slide slightly to the rear and riding the slide forward so as not to shut forcefully on an empty chamber.

Disassembling the Glock Pistol

NOTE- Place the pistol's parts on a flat, clean surface with the muzzle oriented in a safe direction.

When the operator begins to disassemble the pistol, it should be done in the following order:

Field Strip-

    A. Clear the pistol and leave the magazine out.

    B. To remove the slide:

Figure 2-6
Trigger in the forward and ready position

    1. Pull back slide to release slide stop lever and close action to ensure it is in the cocked position (Figure 2-6).

Figure 2-7
Trigger in the rear and fired position

2. Point the pistol in a safe direction and then pull the trigger. You will hear the firing pin move forward (Figure 2-7).

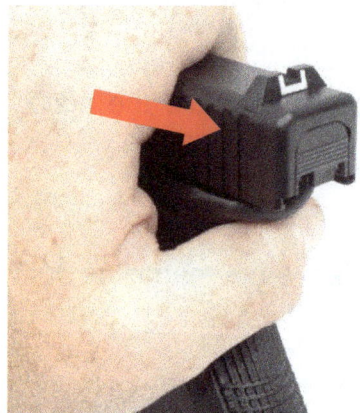

Figure 2-8
Pull the slide slightly out of battery.

3. Hold the pistol in either hand so that four fingers grasp the top of the slide and the thumb is under the tang of frame. With these four fingers, pull and hold the slide back approximately 1/10 inch (Figure 2-8).

Figure 2-9
Pull down on slide lock.

4. Simultaneously, pull down and hold both sides of the slide lock using the thumb and index finger of your free hand (Figure 2-9).

Figure 2-10a
Start to remove the slide.

Figure 2-10b
Completely remove it from frame.

5. Push the slide forward until it is fully separated from the receiver (Figures 2-10a and 2-10b).

C. Remove the recoil spring assembly and barrel.

Figure 2-11
Hold the slide with sights down.

1. Hold the slide by its milled grooves, sight pointed down (Figure 2-11).

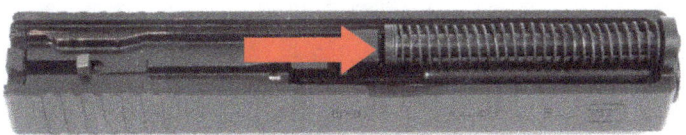
Figure 2-12a
Press in on the recoil spring assembly.

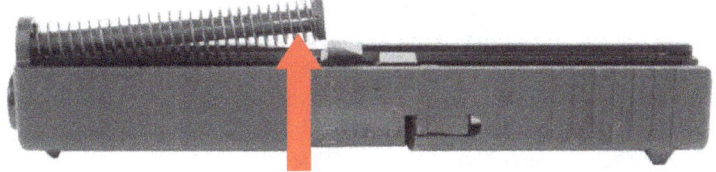
Figure 2-12b
Lift out the recoil spring assembly.

2. Push the recoil spring assembly slightly forward (towards muzzle – Figure 2-12a) while lifting it away from the barrel (Figure 2-12b).

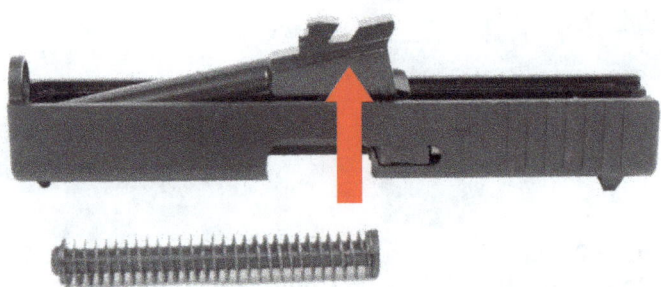

Figure 2-13
Lift the barrel out of the slide.

3. Lift the barrel from the slide up and back out of the frame (Figure 2-13).

Figure 2-14
Field-stripped Glock pistol

1- Slide
2- Barrel
3- Recoil spring assembly
4- Frame
5- Magazine

Disassemble the Glock magazine

A. Ensure the magazine is empty.

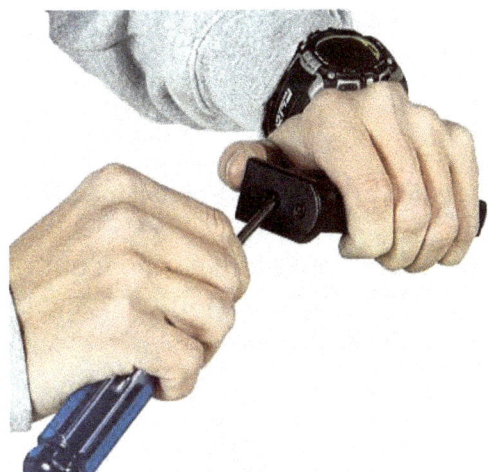

Figure 2-15
Removing the magazine floorplate

B. With a Glock punch or small screwdriver, depress the locking plate under the magazine floorplate (Figure 2-15).

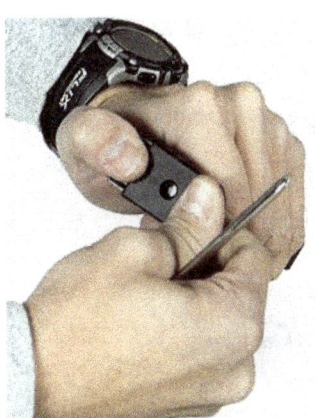

Figure 2-16
Slide the magazine floorplate off.
NOTE- Be sure to maintain pressure on the locking plate.

C. Carefully slide the floorplate off the magazine base while maintaining positive pressure onto the locking plate, which is under spring pressure (Figure 2-16).

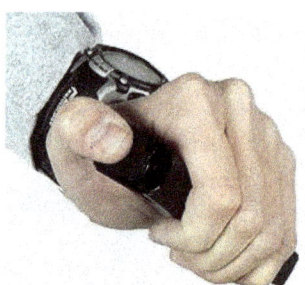

Figure 2-17
Maintain pressure on the locking plate.

D. Begin to let up on the locking plate and control the expansion of the magazine spring; point the bottom of the magazine away from you as you do this (Figures 2-17 and 2-18).

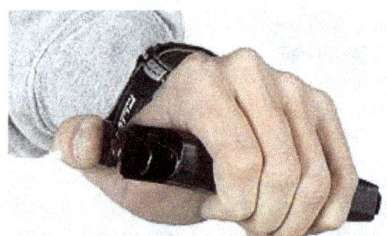

Figure 2-18
Remove the magazine spring from the magazine body.

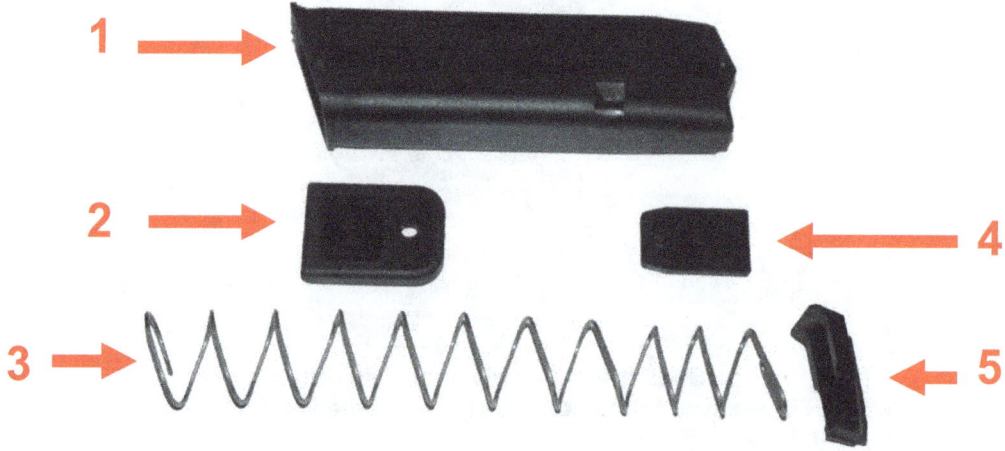

Figure 2-19
Disassembled magazine

1- Magazine Body
2- Floorplate
3- Spring
4- Locking Plate
5- Follower

E. Once disassembled (Figure 2-19), clean prior to reassembling.

Inspecting the Glock

Once the pistol is disassembled and cleaned, it should be thoroughly inspected for damage.

This inspection is for a **field-stripped pistol**:

A. Barrel
   a. Barrel bulged
   b. Cracks at muzzle and or chamber
   c. Longitudinal cracks
   d. Condition of locking lugs

B. Slide
   a. Sights and/or night sights inspection
   b. Front sight pin or screw present
   c. Condition of the grooves
   d. Guide ring
   e. Cracks, especially under the ejection port
   f. Slide stop lever notch
   g. Brass deposits – clean
   h. Extractor clearance – clean

C. Receiver
   a. Magazine catch
   b. Receiver cracks
   c. Slide stop lever tension
   d. Correct ejector
   e. Condition of rails
   f. Slide lock (up and to the rear)

D. Recoil Spring Assembly – inspect for cracked guide rod.

Figure 2-20
Glock tool used for detailed disassembly

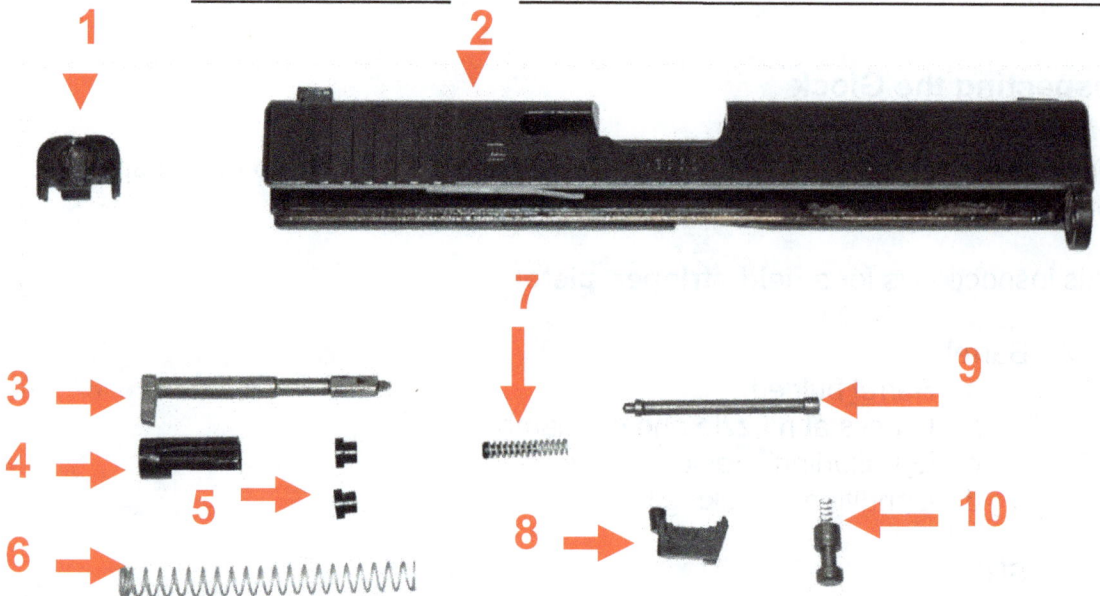

Figure 2-21
Detail-stripped Glock slide assembly

1- Slide cover plate
2- Slide
3- Firing pin
4- Channel liner
5- Spring cups
6- Firing pin spring
7- Extractor depressor plunger spring
8- Extractor
9- Extractor depressor plunger
10- Firing pin safety and spring

Practical Guide to the Operational Use of the **Glock Pistol**

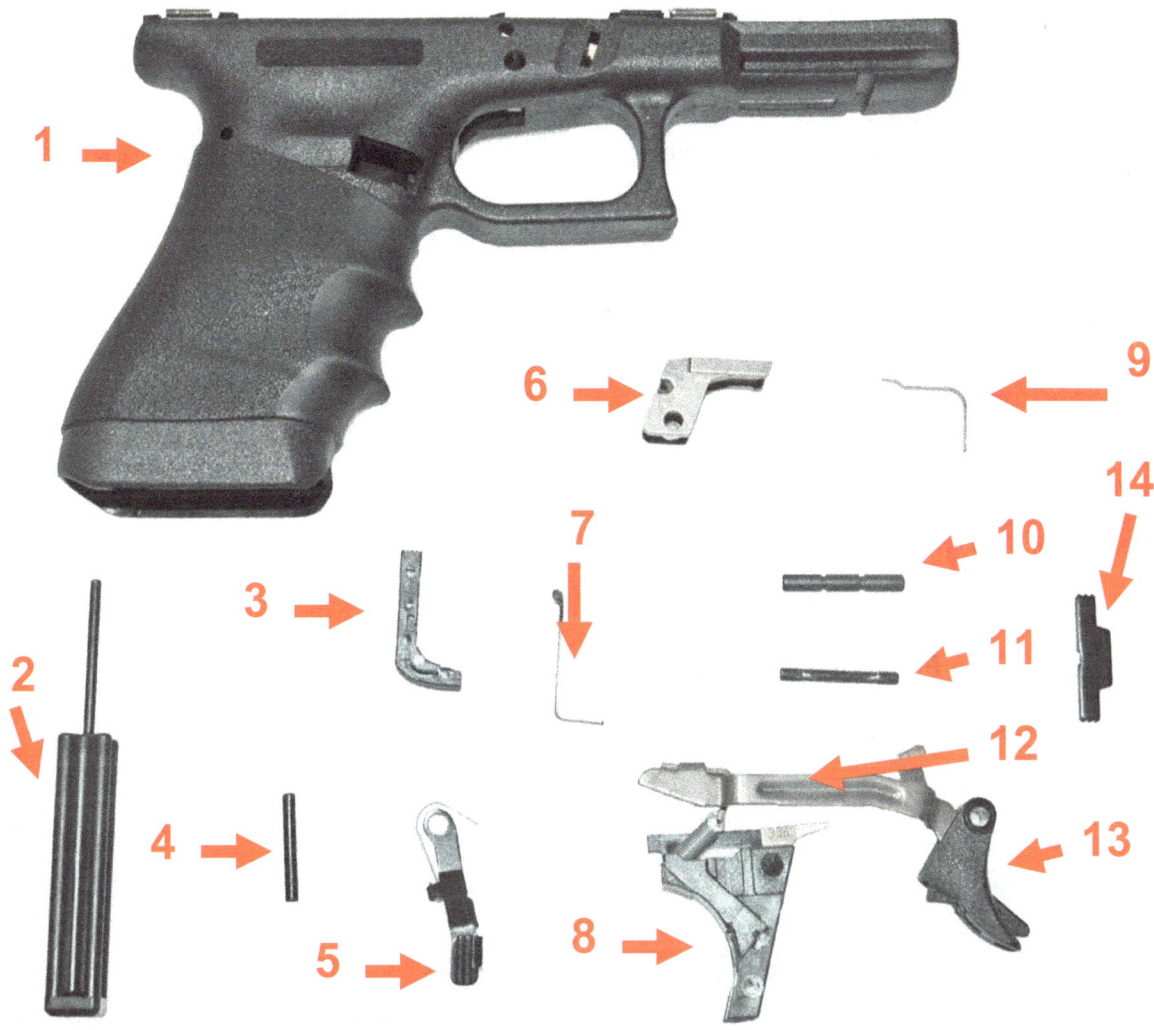

Figure 2-22
Detail-stripped Glock receiver

1- Receiver
2- Glock disassembly tool
3- Magazine catch
4- Trigger housing pin
5- Slide stop and spring

6- Locking block
7- Connector
8- Trigger mechanism housing
9- Slide lock spring
10- Trigger pin

11- Locking block pin
12- Trigger bar
13- Trigger
14- Slide lock

This inspection is for a **detail-stripped pistol,** which is further broken down from the typical field strip. You should be properly trained to perform the detailed disassembly of the pistol by a qualified instructor gunsmith. Look for any obvious cracks, dents, or excessive wear on the parts listed below prior to reassembly.

A. Slide Cover Plate

B. Firing Pin Assembly
   a. Upgrade present
   b. Correct firing pin

  c. Nose chipped or broken?
  d. Firing pin spring cups
  e. Firing pin spring
  f. Spacer sleeve
  g. Firing pin channel liner

C. Extractor Depressor Plunger Assembly
  a. Installed properly
  b. Spring straight and undamaged
  c. Correct spring-loaded bearing

D. Extractor
  a. Upgrade present
  b. Condition of extractor

E. Firing Pin Safety
  a. Upgrade present
  b. Firing pin safety spring in place
  c. Firing pin safety test

F. Locking Block Pin – upgraded

G. Trigger Pin

H. Locking Block

I. Trigger Spring – installed correctly with proper connector

J. Trigger with Trigger Bar
  a. Correct for the pistol
  b. Unusual wear

K. Trigger Mechanism Housing
  a. Ejector condition
  b. Connector tight

L. Magazine
  a. Tube – lips damaged
  b. Spring – correct and undamaged
  c. Follower – cracked or damaged
  d. Correct for pistol

Once the pistol is reassembled, perform an inspection of the following:

A. External visual inspection – overall condition

B. Trigger safety check (Press the sides of the trigger to the rear without disengaging the trigger safety; trigger should not move.)

C. Trigger pull (You should hear the striker be sprung forward; maintain rearward pressure on the trigger and do step D.)

D. Lock slide to the rear and release.

E. Trigger reset check (Release the trigger slowly to hear the reset "click.")

F. Does an empty magazine lock the slide back?

G. Are component parts correct (all parts are for the model of pistol)?

H. Engagement (Check the engagement of the striker to the cruciform with an inspection (orange) rear cover plate.)

Points-
- Do not disassemble the pistol past your ability to reassemble it so it will function properly.
- Do not use the New York trigger spring with an 8 lb. (+) connector. The weapon will not fire with this combination of parts.

Practical Guide to the Operational Use of the **Glock Pistol**

Reassembling the Field-stripped Glock Pistol

A. If you did not inspect the pistol parts during the cleaning, an inspection should be done during the reassembly.

B. To reassemble the Glock:

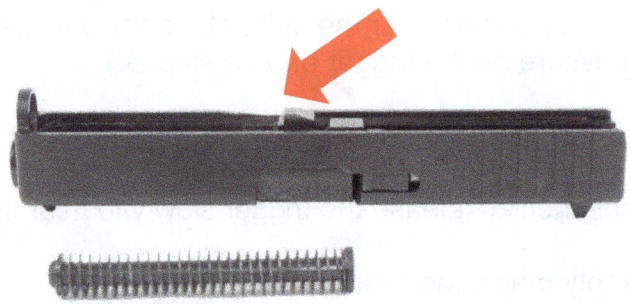

Figure 2-23
Insert the barrel into the slide with the locking lugs up.

1. Insert the barrel (muzzle first) into the slide – down and into the frame (Figure 2-23). Slide the barrel fully to the rear once fully down in the slide.

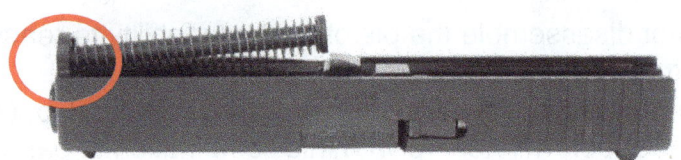

Figure 2-24
Insert the recoil spring assembly into the front of the slide.

2. Insert the recoil spring assembly front end (rounded) into the circular front section of the slide (Figure 2-24).

Figure 2-25
Recoil spring assembly properly installed into the slide

3. Push the recoil spring assembly towards the muzzle slightly and place the rear of the assembly into the rounded cutout on the barrel (Figure 2-25). The assembly will be retained through its

spring tension if properly placed. Do not leave it on the flat non-rounded cutout.

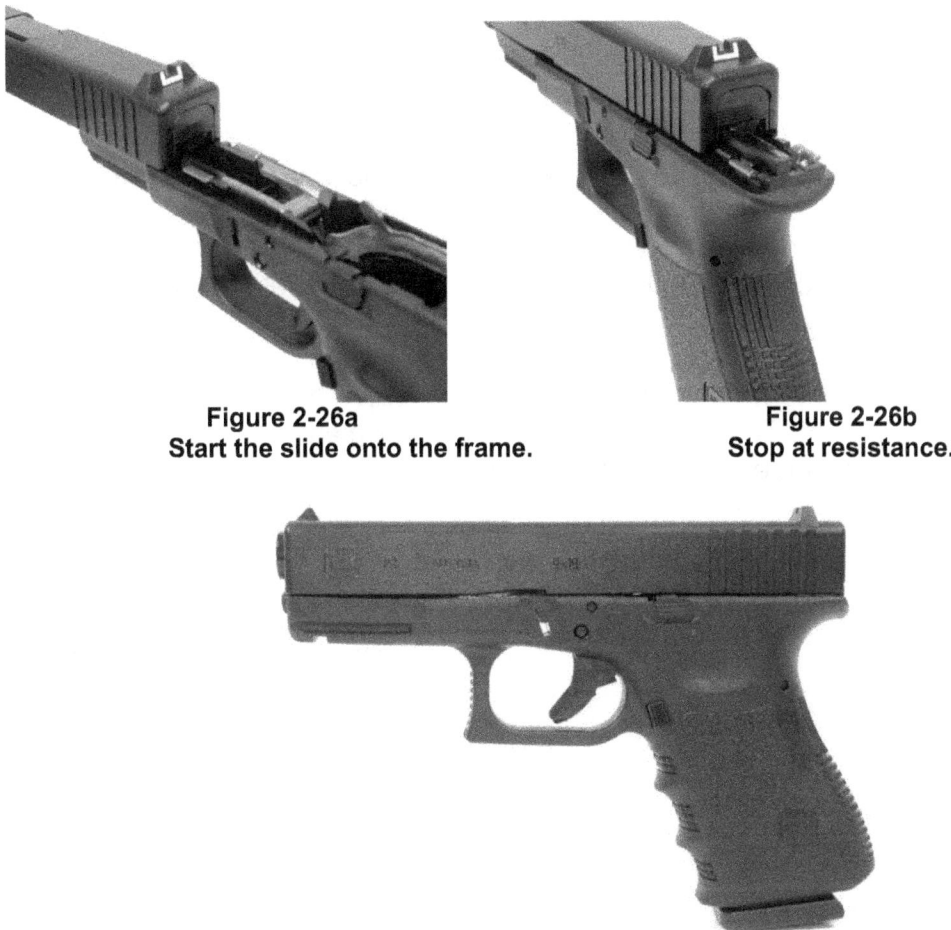

Figure 2-26a
Start the slide onto the frame.

Figure 2-26b
Stop at resistance.

Figure 2-26c
Slide properly installed on the frame

4. Turn the slide over so the sights are up and align the front rails on the receiver with the slide cutouts on the rear of the slide. Once the slide is aligned, pull the slide along the top of the receiver and to the full rearward position. Ease the slide forward and check for proper lock up. Slide should return to in-battery position. (Figures 2-26a-c)

Performing a Function Check on the Glock Pistol

A. Check that all pins are inserted and centered in the receiver.

B. Pull trigger; hold your finger outside the trigger guard, cycle the slide quickly again, and check if trigger is in forward position.

C. Pull trigger, hold trigger to rear, and cycle slide quickly. Release trigger slowly and check trigger safety engagement.

D. Shake the gun forward and backward with the trigger held to the rear. Listen to see if firing pin moves freely.

E. Check engagement of firing pin with trigger bar. There should be at least 2/3 engagement. To make an inspection cover plate, take standard cover plate and grind off area below the metal liner.

Safeties on a Glock

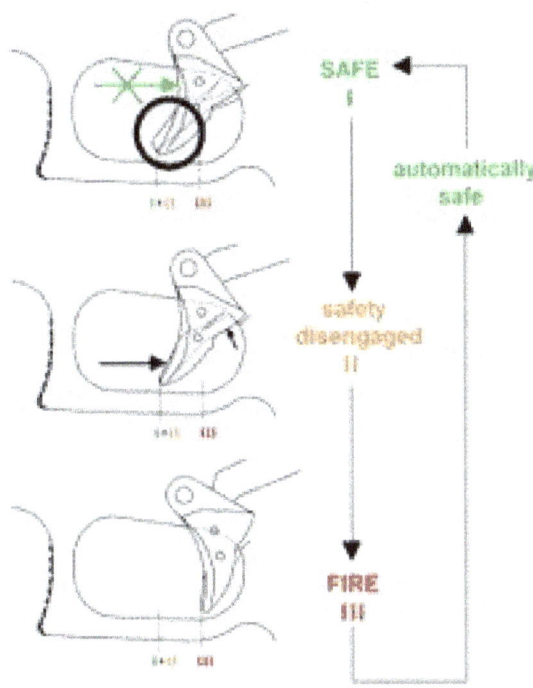

Figure 2-27
Trigger safety explained

A. Trigger Safety

The trigger safety is incorporated into the trigger in the form of a lever and in its normal position prevents the trigger from moving rearward. To fire the pistol, the trigger safety as well as the trigger itself must be deliberately pressed at the same time. If the trigger safety is not depressed, the trigger will not move to the rear, and the pistol will not fire. The trigger safety is designed to prevent accidental firing if the pistol is dropped or subjected to an off-center lateral pressure or similar force (Figure 2-27).

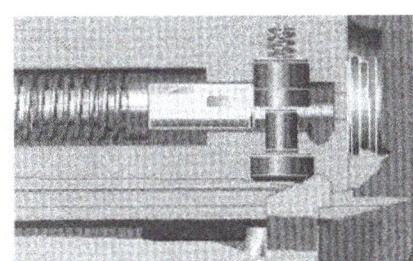
Figure 2-28a

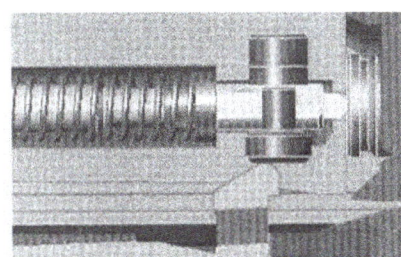
Figure 2-28b

Figure 2-28c
Firing pin safety

B. Firing Pin Safety

The spring-loaded firing pin safety projects into the firing pin cutout and mechanically blocks the firing pin in the ready condition. When the trigger is pulled to the rear, an extension of the trigger bar pushes the firing pin safety upwards, clearing the firing pin channel. During the cycling process, the firing pin safety automatically engages with the help of the firing pin safety spring. The firing pin safety is mainly designed to avoid accidental firing should extreme forces allow a separation of slide and receiver assembly (Figures 2-28a to 2-28c).

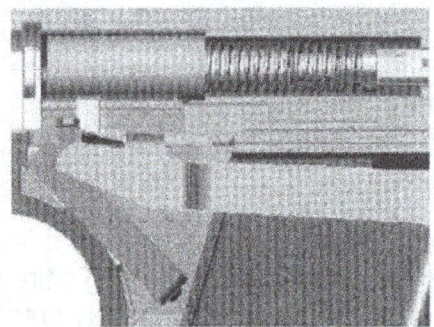 

Figure 2-29
Drop safety

C. Drop Safety

This refers to the safety function of the trigger mechanism housing. The rear part of the trigger bar, which has a cruciform shape, rests with its wings in the loaded/ready position on a safety ramp located in the trigger mechanism housing. When the shooter pulls the trigger to the rear to the pressure point and beyond, the trigger bar starts to leave the safety ramp, being lead downwards and further backwards by the connector and finally separating from the firing pin. During the cycling process of the pistol, the connector is pushed inward by a ramp in the slide, releasing the trigger bar, which is lifted with the help of the trigger spring and caught by the firing pin. This action pushes the trigger bar forward and onto the safety ramp again (Figure 2-29).

Sights

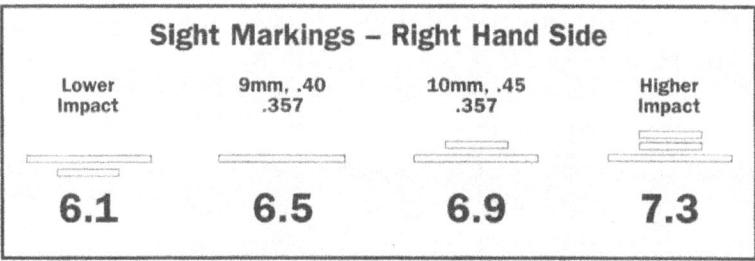

Figure 2-30 Rear Sight Markings

The Glock has four different height rear sights. Each size change will shift point of impact approximately 3 inches at 25 yards (Figure 2-30).

Front Sight Installation (Figure 2-31):
1. Insert new front sight into the front sight slot and press it flush with the top surface of the slide.
2. The new front sight should be placed on a smooth wood or plastic surface after it has been inserted into the slide to be sure it is not pushed out of the slide when inserting the fixing pin.
3. Insert a fixing pin in the slot in the base of the front sight, by hand or with the aid of needle-nose pliers.
4. With a flat screwdriver, push the fixing pin into the base of the front sight.
5. Make sure that the fixing pin is just below the edge of the sight.

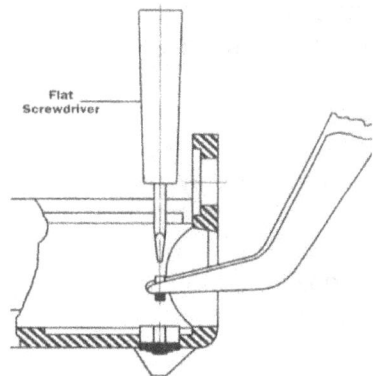

Figure 2-31 Front Sight Installation

Front Night Sight Installation:
Position the front sight in slot, apply thread adhesive to thread, and tighten screw snug. Do not over tighten, or the screw will break. Use a 3/16" nut driver to tighten the screw.

Troubleshooting

When diagnosing malfunctions with the pistol, always start with the simplest and most likely cause. Remember the acronym **SAMM-**

> **S**hooter (improper technique)
> **A**mmunition (incorrect or out of specification)
> **M**aintenance (dirty, unlubricated, or over-lubricated)
> **M**echanical (broken or worn part)

These are the causes of malfunctions in the order they are most likely to occur.

PROBLEM	PROBABLE CAUSES	CORRECTION
Failure to extract	Extractor worn/broken/missing	Replace.
	Overpowered or underpowered	Change ammunition.
	Defective ammunition	
	Dirt under extractor claw	Clean extractor and check.
	Dirty chamber	Clean chamber.
	Shooting with an unlocked wrist	Lock wrists properly.
Failure to eject	Broken or damaged ejector	Replace trigger mechanism housing with ejector.
	Underpowered ammunition	Change ammunition.
	Dirty chamber	Clean chamber.
	Shooting with an unlocked wrist	Lock wrists properly.
	Lack of lubrication	Lubricate as directed.
	Dirty pistol	Clean and lubricate.
Failure to feed	Magazine not properly inserted	Reinsert magazine.
	Underpowered ammunition	Change ammunition.
	Dirty chamber	Clean chamber.
	Weak magazine spring	Replace.
	Dirty chamber	Clean chamber.
	Tight extractor	Replace or clean.
	Shooting with an unlocked wrist	Lock wrists properly.
	Deformed magazine	Replace magazine.
	Weak recoil spring	Replace.
Slide fails to lock open on last round	Magazine follower broken	Replace follower.
	Dirty magazine	Clean.
	Weak magazine spring	Replace.
	Worn slide stop lever notch	Replace.
	Dirty pistol	Clean.
	Lack of lubrication	Lubricate as directed.
	Deformed magazine	Replace magazine.

	Trigger pin inserted too far	The trigger pin may be inserted too far to the left. This can cause the spring on the slide stop lever to bind. Check to see if the slide stop lever moves freely; if not, press the trigger pin slightly to the right until the slide stop lever moves freely.
	Improper grip	Thumb may be depressing the slide stop during firing; reposition thumb.
	Underpowered ammunition	Change ammunition.
	Shooting with an unlocked wrist	Lock wrists properly.
Failure to fire	Slide out of battery due to:	
	Deformed or defective round	Inspect and replace round.
	Underpowered ammunition	Change ammunition.
	Damaged or weak recoil spring	Replace.
	Damaged recoil spring guide	Replace assembly.
	Mating surfaces of barrel, slide, and receiver excessively dirty	Field strip and clean.
	Dirty gun or obstructed chamber	Clean.
	Shooting with an unlocked wrist	Lock wrists properly.
No primer strike	Worn or broken firing pin tip	Replace.
	Obstructed firing pin channel	Clear.
	Spring cups inverted	Change orientation of cups.
Light, centered strike	Hard primers (SMG ammo)	Change ammunition.
	Obstructed firing pin channel	Remove, inspect, and clean firing pin and firing pin spring. Clean firing pin channel.
Light off-centered strike	Tight extractor	Replace.
	Dirty pistol	Clean.
	Slide lock reversed or not beveled	Replace.
Inconsistent trigger	Connector loose in housing	Replace housing.
	Pistol excessively dirty	Field strip and clean.
	Wrong trigger bar	Replace.
	Connector needs lubrication	Lubricate.
	Trigger bar is bent or damaged	Replace trigger bar.
Trigger safety fails to return to engaged (forward) position	Improperly stored in original box with trigger in full forward position (trigger safety fully depressed)	Replace trigger bar. When stored in original box, pistol must be unloaded, trigger in back position.

Firing pin safety fails	Damaged, worn, or defective firing pin spring	Replace damaged part.
Locks open early	Improper hand/thumb position	Grip properly.
	Reverse tension on slide stop lever spring	Replace.
	Damaged slide stop lever	Replace.

Section 3

Operation and Function

Loading the Glock Magazine

A. Ensure you have the correct caliber for the pistol you are shooting. Inspect it for uniformity, cleanliness, and serviceability. Check all cartridges for undented primers and use only issued ammunition.

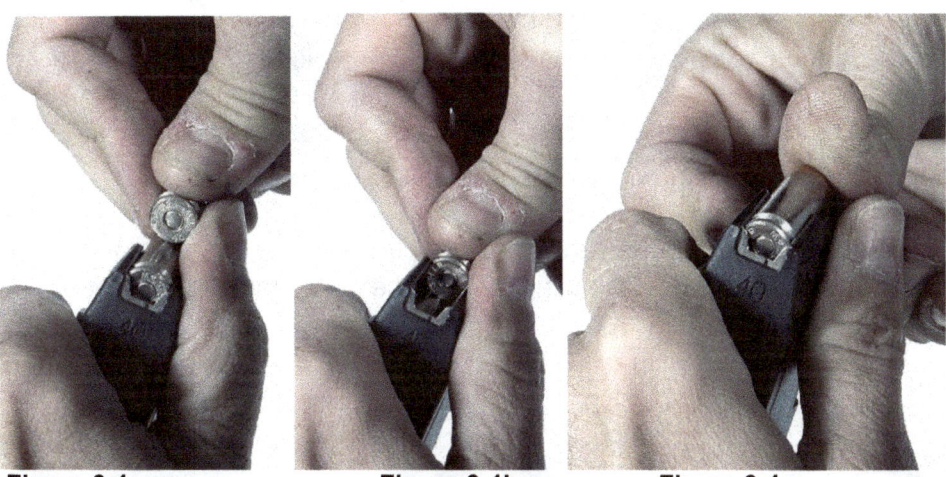

Figure 3-1a   **Figure 3-1b**   **Figure 3-1c**
Loading the Glock magazine

B. Use your non-dominant hand to hold the magazine with the rounded front of the magazine towards your fingertips. Your non-dominant thumb is used as a guide so as not to let the cartridge roll off the follower or other cartridges (Figure 3-1a). With your dominant hand, one at a time, begin with the base of the cartridge at the front of the magazine follower and press the cartridge down and back to insert (Figures 3-1b and 3-1c).

C. The Glock magazines can hold various different round counts, but due to overloading of the spring, do not carry the pistol loaded to capacity for long periods of time. Load the appropriate number of rounds, and then load the chamber, relieving the spring tension by one round. Placing a loose cartridge in the chamber and releasing the slide stop can cause damage to the extractor, so load the chamber from the magazine only.

Loading the Glock Pistol

A. With the pistol pointed in a safe direction:

Figure 3-2 Locking the slide to the rear

B. Lock the slide to the rear by pulling the slide to the rear and pressing up on the slide stop (Figure 3-2). Once it is engaged, release the slide tension.

Figure 3-3a   **Figure 3-3b**   **Figure 3-3c**
Inserting the magazine into the magazine well

C. Insert the loaded magazine into the magazine well (Figures 3-3a and 3-3b). Fully seat the magazine with the heel of the hand to ensure it is locked in by the magazine catch (Figure 3-3c).

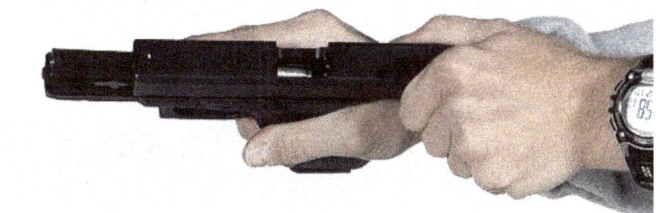

Figure 3-4a Pull the slide to the rear.

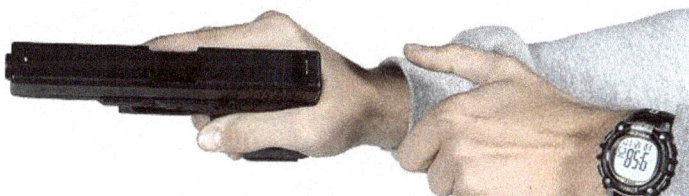

Figure 3-4b Release the slide.

D. Pull the slide by gripping the serrations on the rear of the slide (not over the ejection port) to the rear and release, allowing it to slam shut by its own spring tension (Figures 3-4a and 3-4b). To ensure that a round has been chambered, either remove the magazine to observe that one less round is in the counting window on the back of the magazine or perform a press check to observe the chambered casing through the ejection port. An alternative method of closing the slide to load is to press down on the slide stop and allow it to shut by its own spring tension. Ensure the slide is in battery (fully forward). Do not close the slide by pressing down on the slide stop unless there are cartridges in the magazine.

E. As the Glock is a safe action pistol, there are no external safeties to engage. The internal safeties are all engaged.

Firing the Glock Pistol

Figure 3-5 Glock firing position

A. Orient downrange in the direction of your targets or towards the threat (Figure 3-5).

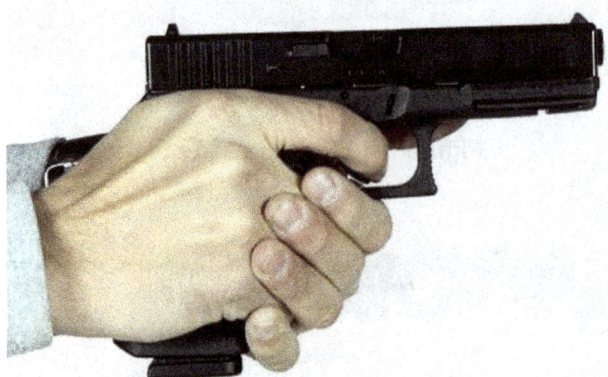

Figure 3-6 Proper grip

B. As you orient your sights onto the target, press the trigger straight back so as not to interrupt the sight picture (Figure 3-6). As the Glock is a safe action pistol, you will notice your first shot will have a heavier trigger pressure than subsequent shots that are single action (hammer already to the rear). Remember to perform proper follow through and recovery, and you should practice proper trigger reset to ensure light trigger pressure needed for subsequent shots.

C. When you have completed firing the pistol, remove your finger from the trigger and place it outside of the trigger guard.

Section 4

Performance Problems

Malfunction and Immediate Action Procedures

Malfunctions are usually preventable through good practices, but they may still occur out of the blue from time to time. Of course, you hope it is on the practice range, but you should treat each one as though you are in a life-or-death situation. Practicing proper and effective corrective actions will allow you to be more confident in your pistol handling. In stressful situations, you can become much more stressed due to an unforeseen malfunction that is easy to correct. I have observed many shooters who perceive themselves to be experienced, but when they encounter a stovepipe, they nearly disassemble the pistol rather than sweep it out and continue.

Malfunction drills must fix the problem 100% of the time (excluding a weapon stoppage – broken weapon) the first time performed. You must look at the pistol and identify the problem (obviously the pistol is not functioning as you need it to, so you must transition to another weapon or rectify the situation); it is a non-functioning weapon at this point – fix it.

You should always practice taking a covered position to correct malfunctions with considerations on how you operate.

The following pages in this chapter describe and detail corrective actions for the various malfunctions that may be encountered.

NOTE: The failure-to-go-into-battery malfunction, when your slide does not fully return forward when cycling a round, is always rectified in the same manner, no matter which hand is being used. This malfunction is usually induced when loading and failing to allow the full recoil spring tension to shut the slide.

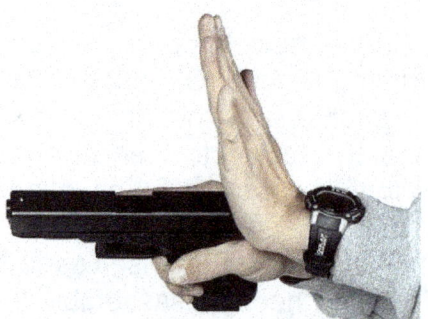

Figure 4-1 Seating the slide

To fix a failure-to-go-into-battery malfunction, you must ensure your finger is off the trigger and outside the trigger guard, and then slap the back of the slide with the heel of the non-firing hand (Figure 4-1). If you are shooting while wounded, then you will use your chest or equipment to force the slide forward into battery.

FAILURE TO FIRE: This malfunction occurs when the operator has loaded a dud cartridge or failed to load the chamber. The universal fix-all for this is the "Slap, Rack, Bang" technique.

SYMPTOM – You perform a full presentation to shoot and hear and feel the hammer strike, but the weapon does not fire.

Figure 4-2 Slap

1. **SLAP** the bottom of the magazine with a hard palm (fingers extended) to ensure it is fully seated and locked in (Figure 4-2).

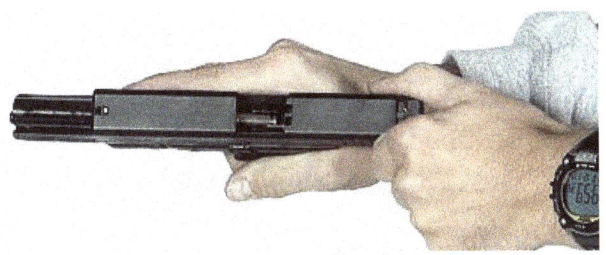

Figure 4-3 Rack

2. **RACK** the slide fully to the rear and release it to shut by its own recoil spring tension. You can pivot the slide toward your non-firing hand to assist in racking the slide to the rear; maintain muzzle to threat orientation (Figure 4-3).

Figure 4-4 Ready/Bang

3. **READY/BANG** or re-present and prepare to fire the shot as you intended before the malfunction if your situation dictates that action (Figure 4-4).

FAILURE TO EJECT: This malfunction (commonly called a "stovepipe") is created usually by the slide being retarded (by not setting one's wrists – "limp wristing") in its rearward movement to rechamber the next round or broken ejector. This malfunction can also be induced by an excessively dirty extractor which does not fully grip the rim of the cartridge during ejection. This malfunction is easily corrected by sweeping the expended case from the port. The corrective action is the same for vertical and horizontal stovepipes.

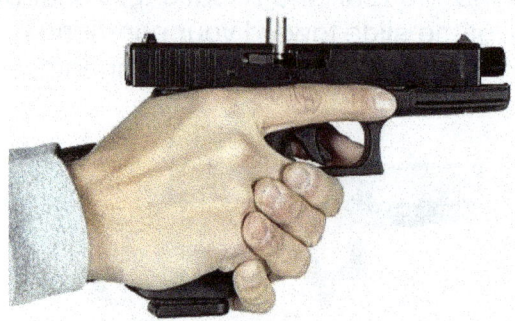

Figure 4-5 Stovepipe

SYMPTOM – You are in the act of shooting a multiple-round engagement, and you notice you cannot see your front sight for a piece of brass is in the way, you feel the slide did not fully close, and/or you have a soft mushy trigger.

Figure 4-6a Reach across   **Figure 4-6b Rearward sweep**

With the non-firing hand, extend your fingers, and with fingers joined, reach over the slide. (DO NOT SWEEP YOUR HAND IN FRONT OF THE MUZZLE.) Roll your fingers over the top of the slide with a firm, vigorous sweeping motion to the rear against the stuck casing to sweep it free (Figures 4-6a and 4-6b). Do not sweep too far as you have to take more time to regrip and present.

Once the casing is no longer pinched by the slide, the slide will continue to seat the next round, and you are now ready to continue the engagement. Many inexperienced shooters do too much to correct this simple malfunction. **Ensure you do not work the slide fully to the rear when sweeping the empty casing; this action could induce a double feed as the chamber is already loaded.** Continue the engagement as your situation dictates.

NOTE: You must always roll your fingers across so that whichever malfunction you encounter, vertical or horizontal, you will clear it with one sweep.

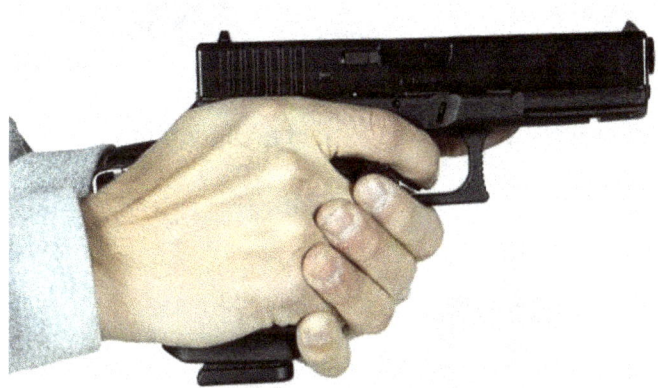

Figure 4-7 Present and fire

FAILURE TO EXTRACT: This malfunction (commonly called a "double feed") is created when the spent casing is not extracted from the chamber, and the next round to be loaded is rammed from the magazine into the rear of the stuck casing (Figures 4-8 and 4-9). This malfunction is a serious one since more complicated dexterity is needed to correct it and, of course, to do it quickly. Below is the breakdown of the corrective action to restore your pistol back to operation.

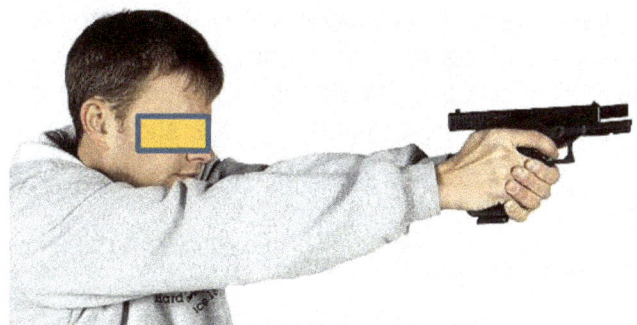

Figure 4-8 Failure to extract

SYMPTOM – You are shooting a multiple-shot engagement and notice your slide did not go forward, you have a soft mushy trigger, and the pistol will not fire (Figures 4-8 and 4-9).

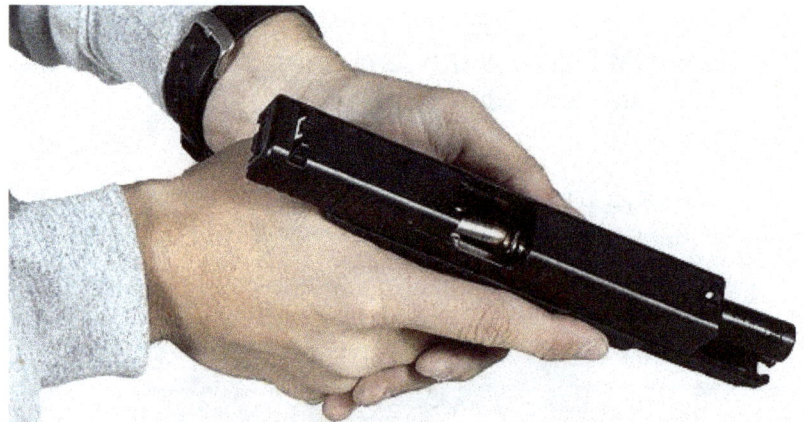

Figure 4-9 Failure to extract malfunction

Figure 4-10 Step one of corrective actions

STEP ONE - With your finger off the trigger, rotate the pistol in your firing hand so you may engage the slide stop with your firing-hand thumb. With the non-firing hand, rack the slide to the rear and lock it with the slide stop by pushing it up into the notch, and let the recoil spring tension hold the slide stop in the notch (Figure 4-10).

Practical Guide to the Operational Use of the **Glock Pistol**

Figure 4-11 Step two of corrective actions

STEP TWO - Remove the magazine from the pistol (Figure 4-11).

Figure 4-12 Step three of corrective actions

STEP THREE - Rack the slide to the rear at least two times to ensure the casing is extracted and ejected from the pistol (Figure 4-12). As you are doing this step, observe the casing being ejected and allow the slide to use its force to shut each time it is pulled to the rear. You can rotate the slide towards your non-firing hand to assist in working the slide to the rear.

Practical Guide to the Operational Use of the **Glock Pistol**

Figure 4-13 Step four of corrective actions

STEP FOUR - Properly insert and seat a loaded magazine with a hard palm (Figure 4-13).

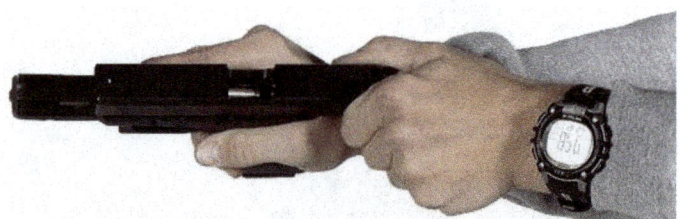

Figure 4-14 Step five of corrective actions

STEP FIVE - Rack the slide fully to the rear and release it to close by its own spring tension (Figure 4-14). Your pistol is now ready to continue the engagement. You can rotate the slide towards your non-firing hand to assist in working the slide to the rear.

Figure 4-15 Step six of corrective actions

STEP SIX - Continue the engagement as the situation dictates (Figure 4-15).

NOTE: Correcting this malfunction needs to be practiced often since it is the most complicated to do under stress or when you lose dexterity because blood is leaving the extremities.

Appendix A – Accessories for Glock Pistols

Jentra Plug- Keeps dirt, dust, and snow out of grip frame. Snaps into the open pocket at the rear of the Glock grip frame for a cleaner appearance, plus keeps dust, dirt, snow, and water out of the gun. Creates a perfect location for adding extra weight to competition guns or to counter recoil on lightweight-carry guns. Easily removed, it does not alter the pistol.

Available in three sizes:
Small (Glock 26, 27, 33; does not fit 29 & 30)
Regular (Glock 17, 19, 20-25, 31, 32, 34, 35)
Glock 29 & 30

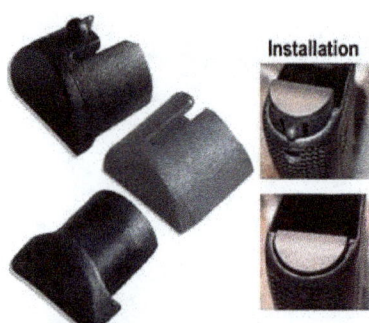

Figure A-1 Jentra Plug

Skyline Tools Glock Carry Clip- Easy-to-install, spring-steel belt clip eliminates the holster, reduces bulk, improves concealment, and gives a sleeker profile. Clip, mounted on replacement slide cover plate, extends along the right or left side of the slide. Carry your pistol conveniently tucked in your waistband, pocket, or boot. This clip does not interfere with slide function. No-gunsmith installation necessary and can be installed on either side of your pistol. Use in conjunction with the Saf-T-Blok listed below.

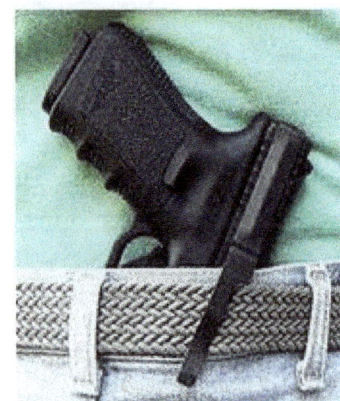

Figure A-2 Skyline Glock Carry Clip

Saf-T-Blok- Prevents unintentional discharges and discourages unauthorized use.

Plastic drop-in trigger-block safety fits behind the trigger to prevent accidental discharges. The color matches Glock's finish, making it virtually unnoticeable. Designed to frustrate and delay unauthorized personnel that might try to fire the weapon. Snaps easily into place and ejects instantly for use.

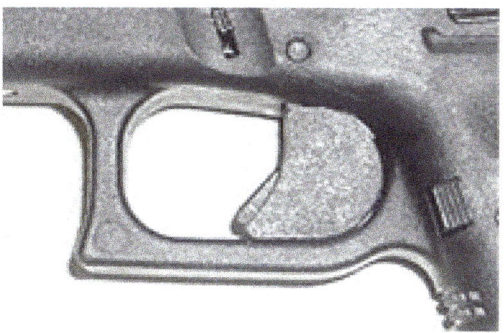

Figure A-3 Saf-T-Blok

Figure A-4 Ameriglo Tritium Sights

Figure A-5 Ameriglo Tritium Sights

Figure A-6 Wolff Extra Power Spring Kit

Figure A-7 Ghost Glock Armorer Tool Kit

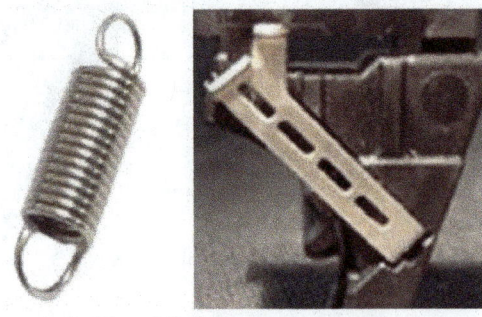

Figure A-8 Ghost 3.5-Pound Ultimate Trigger Kit

Figure A-9 Ghost 5-Pound Tactical Trigger Control Connector

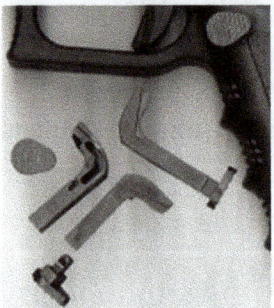

Figure A-10 Ghost Extended Magazine Release

**Figure A-11 Glock Handbook
Item Number VSS-012-005**
www.vig-sec.com

Appendix B – Holsters, Magazine Pouches, and Lights

There are various manufacturers offering better options than the issued leather Glock holster. Fobus, Bladetech, Survival Sheath, and Uncle Mike's all make quality holsters for the Glock pistols.

Holsters

Figure B-1 Blackhawk Level 2 SERPA holster

Figure B-2 Blackhawk Level 3 SERPA light bearing holster

Figure B-3a Fobus Paddle Holster for Glock (GL2)

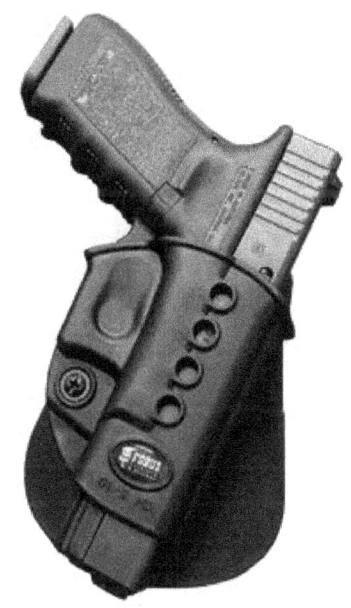

Figure B-3b Fobus New Evolution Holster for Glock

Figure B-4 Fobus Roto Paddle Holster GL2-RP

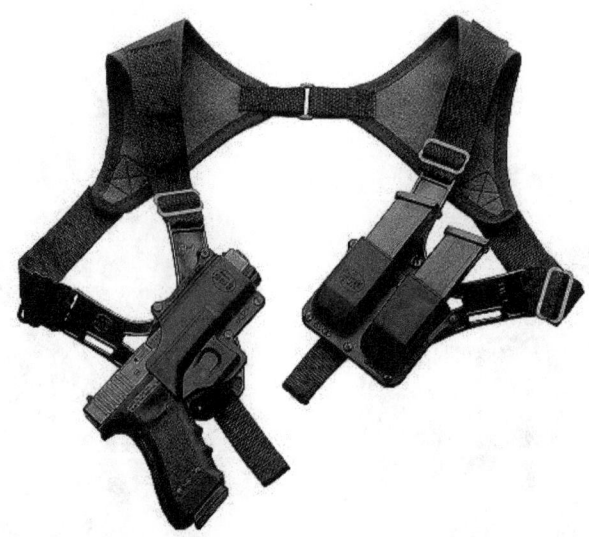

Figure B-5 Roto Shoulder Holster Harness (SHR2 – harness only)

Figure B-6 Universal Vehicle/Home Mount (UVM)

The Fobus roto model can be configured to fit the roto shoulder holster harness (SHR2), the universal vehicle/home mount (UVM), and the drop-leg thigh harness (FOB-TTR, shown above). Glock pistol shown in photos.

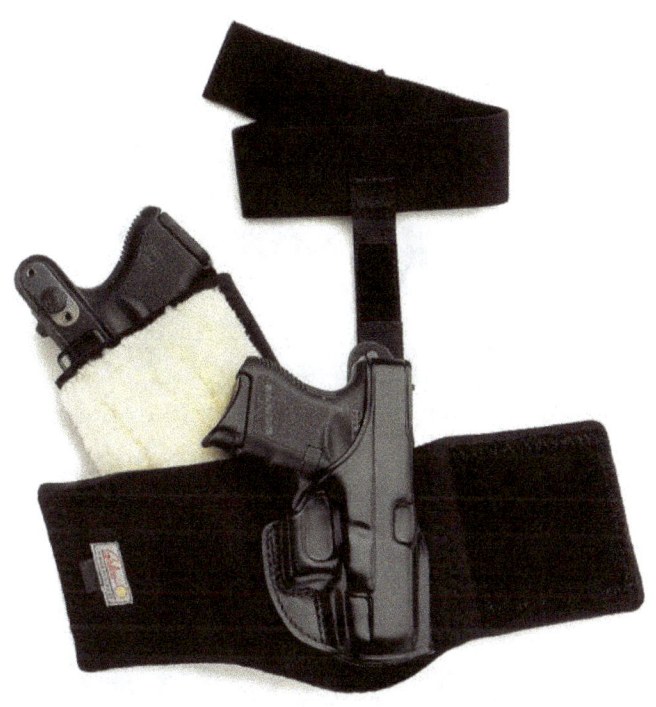

Figure B-7 Galco Ankle Glove Holster (GAL-AG226)

Figure B-8 Galco Ultra Deep Cover Holster (GAL-UDCXX)

Figure B-9 Galco Fletch High Ride Holster (Sig shown) (GAL-FLXX)

Figure B-10 Galco SOB Small of Back Holster (GAL-SOBXX)

Offers an initial tight fit, but once broken in, this holster is a very good daily carry-type holster that is comfortable and retained with the thumb break.

Magazine Pouches

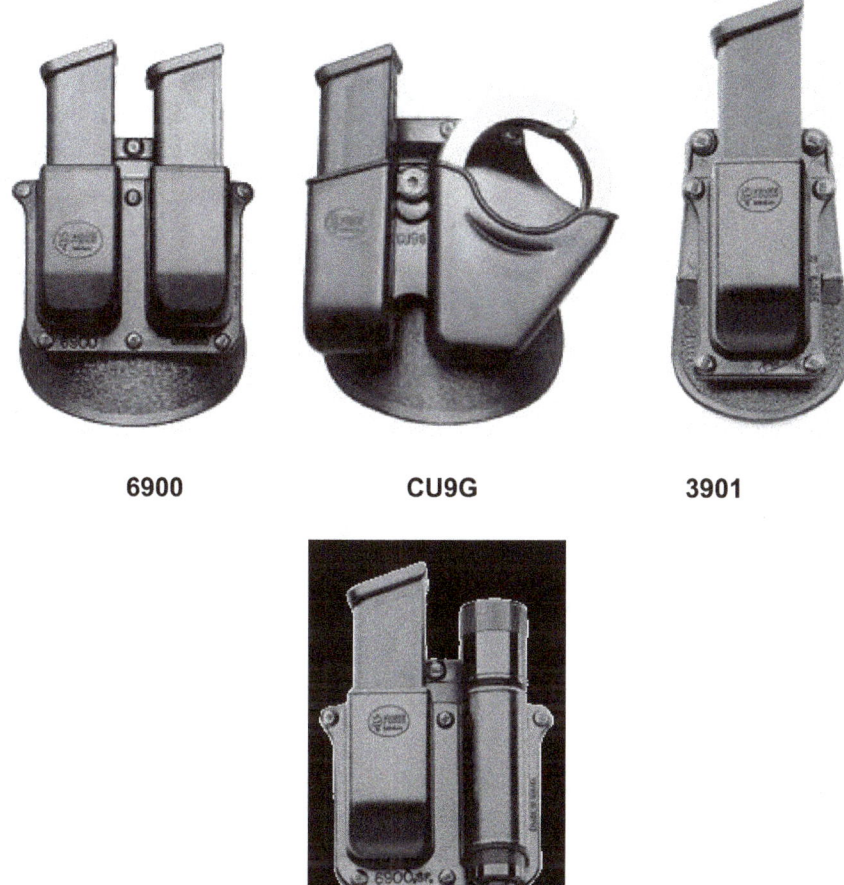

6900   CU9G   3901

SF6900

Figure B-11 Various Fobus magazine pouches

GAL-DMP22B   GAL-UDCMC24

Figure B-12 Various Galco magazine pouches

**Figure B-13 Blackhawk single magazine pouch
410600CBK**

Lights

Figure B-14 Blackhawk Xiphos LED weapon light

The Xiphos NT is a 3-volt rail-mounted LED pistol light boasting over 65 lumens of blinding white LED light at full power. The digitally controlled "smart" circuitry has been programmed to perform different useful functions while at the same time allowing ease of use, under duress, by the end user. These functions include the same "strobing" feature as on the Night-Ops Gladius, enabling the user to disorient a potential adversary and/or "visually distort" the perception of what a potential adversary observes. The "smart" circuitry has been programmed to optimize light output for the entire life of the battery, giving an incredible 2+ hours of continuous light output. The Xiphos NT is designed to be activated with a single hand OR both hands using the ambidextrous digital pressure switch. The switch design is very versatile and intuitive. It can be activated either laterally across the "X" axis of the light (left to right or right to left) OR across the "Y" axis (forward to rear).

Figure B-15 Streamlight M3

Streamlight M3 Lightweight polymer body tactical light with momentary or constant "ON" feature. This model is for Glock pistols with rails and uses two 3- volt lithium batteries. (GLL-001-A1)

Figure B-16 Streamlight M6

Streamlight M-6 Tactical Laser illuminator/gun-mounted tactical light is an integrated laser/white light combo at the price of a laser sight alone. The Streamlight M-6 Tactical Laser Illuminator offers a uniquely integrated high-power visible laser combined with a high-intensity white light in a military-proven design. (TLI-000-A1)

www.ingramcontent.com/pod-product-compliance
Lightning Source LLC
Chambersburg PA
CBHW080524110426
42742CB00017B/3224